MW01094004

Essential Oils for Dogs

The Complete Essential Oils Guide for Your Beloved Family Dog!

Recipes Included

Table of Contents:

Introduction

I want to thank you and congratulate you for downloading the book, *"Essential Oils for Dogs: The Complete Essential Oils Guide for Your Beloved Family Dog! Recipes Included."*

This book contains proven steps and strategies on how to use essential oils to make your beloved family dog become healthier and happier. It serves as your complete guide to essential oils, making you understand how oils can benefit your dog. It gives you a list of essential oils and their therapeutic and medicinal properties so that you know exactly what to use to address your dog's particular health and behavioral problems.

This book gives you a rundown of the dos

and don'ts as they apply to the use of essential oils so you know how to use them effectively. It also tells you what essential oils to avoid as they tend to have adverse effects on your dog's well-being. It even includes effective and easy-to-prepare recipes to help you treat problems affecting your beloved family dog. It is an extremely helpful and exhaustive guide to essential oils.

Thanks again for downloading this book, I hope you enjoy it!

Chapter 1 – An Overview of Essential Oils

What are Essential Oils?

Essential oils are the aromatic, highly concentrated chemical components that exist by nature in plants. They are extracted from the fruit, peel, seeds, roots, bark, twigs, flowers, or leaves of the plant through the process of distillation. They are the "essence" of a particular plant and carry the plant's unique fragrance, chemical features and healing effects.

The use of essential oils in aromatherapy is becoming increasingly popular. People are finding out that these oils promote physical health and emotional well-being. They demonstrate the same healing powers present in the plants where they were extracted. Diluted in base oils, you can apply them to your beloved family dog's body as an alternative treatment that is safe and effective.

Why are Treatments Using Essential Oils Popular?

More and more people are showing their love for their dog by using essential oils to promote their beloved dog's health and sense of well-being. More than just simply using fragrant oils in grooming products or in scented candles, people are using essential oils in a variety of ways to make their pet dog healthier and happier.

Research shows that essential oils have

both therapeutic and medicinal properties. You can help your dog overcome many of his discomforts – ranging from fleas, odor, skin irritation, and motion sickness to behavioral ones like anxiety and hyperactivity. By learning how to use essential oils, you can do more than just make your beloved pet smell good. You can help make his life with you more joyful and productive by helping ease some of the more common problems that he may face.

The use of essential oils is now very popular with people who love their dogs dearly, and this goes beyond using shampoos, conditioners and other essential dog grooming products containing essential oils. The oils are now highly regarded as an essential part of holistic healing treatments – not only for physical problems but for behavioral ones as well.

How Do You Use Essential Oils on your Dog?

You have to dilute the oils before using them. You can choose the carrier vegetable oil you prefer; your options include the more widely preferred sweet almond oil, jojoba oil, and olive oil, among many.

You can apply essential oils through diffusion and inhalation. When you diffuse the fragrance into a room that your pet often stays in, you give him the chance to breathe in the scent in a natural and gentle way. A diffuser combines the essential oils with a heat source like an electric diffuser or some candles. You can use just a few drops of the diluted essential oils. This is enough for the scent to suffuse the room in a lovely and delicate manner.

Leave the diffuser on for about half an hour to effectively evaporate the oils, which the dog inhales and absorbs. Let your pet stay in the room to breathe in the evaporated oils. Do this twice a day for about a week so that your dog will enjoy significant results from the treatment.

Topical application yields the most immediate results. You apply the oils directly on the area where your dog needs it most. You massage the essential oils on the skin, allowing them to penetrate the skin, so that the tiny capillaries can absorb them and move them directly into the bloodstream.

Essential oils can also be ingested. This technique, however, is not as commonly practiced as the first two because it requires a holistic veterinarian to supervise the process. The oils are potent. Careless use of it may result in harming your beloved dog. It is much more prudent for you to use topical application and inhalation if you want your dog to reap significant benefits from the treatment.

How to Introduce Essential Oils to your Dog?

If your pet seems wary of essential oils,

introduce the oils to him gradually. You can diffuse them very delicately at first, then increase the intensity a bit once he gets used to the fragrance. You can also massage a little amount onto your palms and affectionately pet your dog or stroke him in ways that he enjoys.

Smelling the oils conditions your pet to perceive them more positively. This will also allow him to feel comfortable with the scent. Once you think that your pet dog is more responsive to the fragrance, you can then move on to topical application.

Chapter 2 – The Many Benefits of Essential Oils

If you know what essential oils to avoid and which to use for your pet dog, you – and your dog – will love the benefits that come with their use.

Essential oils are naturally occurring. They have all the essential characteristics of the plants from which they were extracted – including their therapeutic and healing properties. They help your pet feel healthier, more energetic, and less prone to the irritating and painful symptoms of certain conditions like arthritis and allergies.

Essential oils are handy, simple and easy to use. You can always keep a small bottle in your purse when you travel with your dog so you can apply a few drops any time a situation warrants it.

They are convenient to apply. You can simply diffuse them in your car or your home so that your pet can enjoy its healing – and soothing – effects. Or you can use topical application, allowing your beloved pet to benefit from the essential oils' properties, as well as from your gentle and loving touch.

There are many reasons to use essential oils on your beloved family dog.

Essential oils facilitate your dog's digestion and calm his stomach. They help cure diarrhea.

Oils help in giving your dog better

skin. They soothe skin irritations and work wonders in repelling ticks and fleas. They calm swelling from insect bites and stings.

Essential oils help your dog recover from sniffles, cough and other respiratory problems.

They help prevent and get rid of body odor – making your dog smell fresh and nice, and his breath, clean and wonderful.

They soothe painful muscles and joints. If your dog suffers from arthritis, he is likely to appreciate the relief that comes with the use of essential oils.

Essential oils have a soothing effect on overworked muscles, stomach discomforts, skin irritation, indigestion, and many more.

They also soothe and calm frayed nerves. They help control adverse emotional conditions. They are useful in curbing hyperactivity. They are an effective antidote to your pet's nervousness, anxiety and grief. They help ease tension and promote a sense of comfort and assurance.

Your pet dog is likely to feel less jittery, less anxious, or less hyperactive when he feels the calming and soothing effects of essential oils.

Chapter 3 - It pays to be cautious

Are Essential Oils Safe for Dogs?

Essential oils come in concentrated form and are, thus, very potent. When you use essential oils for your beloved dog, make sure that you know exactly how to use them properly. Do not use them in more than the recommended amounts. Make sure that you use sweet almond oil, olive oil or some other carrier oils to dilute them.

Different essential oils have different therapeutic and healing properties. Take the time to find out the kind of essential oil, which is best for certain ailments. Used correctly, essential oils are safe for your dog. They are likely to help him recover from certain ailments or problems.

Do not forget to ALWAYS dilute the essential oils prior to use. There are many oils you can use as base oils, including those of sweet almond, hazelnut, sunflower, jojoba, safflower, olive, avocado and grape seed.

Be guided accordingly. Add 15ml or ½ oz. of the carrier base oil of your choice to roughly 8 to 10 drops of essential oil. This translates to between 25 to 30 drops of essential oils for a 240 ml or 8 oz. bottle of shampoo.

Some essential oils – whether you dilute them or not -- are UNSAFE for your dog. Stay away from these essential oils. Make sure to limit your use to essential oils that are proven safe for dogs.

Important Things to Bear in Mind When Using Essential Oils on your Pet

Oral medication for children takes into account the weight of the child in determining the dosage. This is also the case with essential oils and your dog. The size of your dog should be considered in determining the intensity of the essential oil blends, as well as the duration of treatment.

When treating people who have special conditions – pregnant, old, frail, sick – you give special considerations. The same holds true with treating your dog with essential oils.

If you have a small dog, decrease the amount of diluted oil that you use on him. Do the same if you have a puppy, a senior dog, or one who is weak and sickly. Do not use oils if your dog is prone to seizures or episodes of epilepsy

Do not apply the essential oil blend on your dog's genital or anal areas or close to or directly on his nose or eyes.

Your dog is sensitive to essential oils. When you are just introducing the oils to him, make sure to dilute heavily. Then use the diluted potion moderately so that your dog gets the chance to get used to the treatment.

Although there are guidelines regarding the general use of essential oils, remember that every pet is unique and may react differently. Be observant. Assess how your pet responds to the treatment. Be sensible and cautious.

Your dog will not be able to tell you how he is responding to the essential oils treatment. You have to observe his reactions and watch out for signs indicating whether or not he is responding positively or adversely. If he whines, sniffs, scratches, or becomes nervous, you may have to make certain adjustments in your treatment.

Essential oils are helpful for your pet dog to become physically and psychologically fit. You have to understand, though, that these oils are strong and powerful. When used inappropriately, they may have adverse effects. You have to apply the general principles for their safe use.

Over-use is a potential problem with essential oils. Do not be so enthusiastic that you go overboard in using the oils. Your pet dog may have a sensitive sense of smell and react to the inordinate use of the oils by developing allergies or skin irritations. Moderation is essential in the use of these oils. It may be wise to use the oils for no longer than two weeks and then give their use a rest before beginning another period of treatment.

Harmful Essential Oils

There are many essential oils that will prove extremely helpful in caring for your beloved pet. However, on its flipside are essential oils that may prove harmful. The following essential oils are unsafe for your dog:

Yarrow, white thyme, juniper wood, hyssop, camphor, and anise may be toxic and stimulate the uterine. Stay away from these oils, particularly if your dog is pregnant.

Wintergreen and birch have elevated levels of methyl salicylate. Dermal use of these oils may prove harmful. When ingested, these oils may prove noxious – and may even cause death.

Clove leaf and Cassia may cause skin irritation.

Tansy, mustard and horseradish are extremely pungent. Excessive use may be risky, causing dermal pain and irritation.

Pennyroyal repels flea. However, it has also been demonstrated to harm the nerve and kidneys.

There have been findings that the essential oils of wormwood can treat worm infestation. However, they can also cause harm to the kidneys and result in renal failure. Better keep these oils away from your beloved pet.

Chapter 4 –Selecting High-Quality Essential Oils

If you are buying essential oils for the first time, what are the things that you should look out for? There are many suppliers of essential oils; it pays to be discerning when deciding from which store you are going to get your oils.

You should know how to look for first-class essential oils.

Look for oils that come in violet, cobalt, or amber bottles. Oils do not turn rancid over time but they do deteriorate – oxidizing and losing most of their therapeutic properties. While some oils like sandalwood and patchouli improve their fragrance with age, most tend to lose their beautiful and soothing scents. It is thus important to buy essential oils from suppliers who store and handle the oils with care.

It is better to buy oils that come packaged in dark-colored glass bottles, instead of clear ones. Exposure to sunlight tends to have a deteriorative effect on essential oils; it makes them inferior in quality, value and character. Clear-glass bottles do not harm essential oils but they do a poor job of protecting the oils from the damaging effects of sunlight. Dark-colored glass bottles help preserve essential oils so that they keep their therapeutic and aromatic qualities.

Make sure that the bottles have labels containing all the information you need to know. If you are ordering online, check the website for the data. Look at brochures if these are available.

What is the scientific name of the oil? What country does it come from? How was the plant cultivated? How was the oil extracted? Is the oil 100% pure essential oil? It is important to note all these details.

One important thing to understand is that some oils are not as pure as they ought to be. Some oils may have additives or contaminates that may do more harm than good to your pet. Make sure to buy your essential oils from credible and well-respected companies.

When buying essential oils, make sure to get those that are classified as therapeutic-grade and 100% pure. You demonstrate the love you have for your dog by allowing him the therapeutic use of high-grade 100% pure essential oils for healing purposes.

There are less expensive oils that are passed off as "essential." It requires a lot of plant material to produce a small amount of essential oils. A pound of lavender essential oils requires a hundred pounds of the said plant. Because of the cost entailed in extracting essential oils, some companies dilute the oils with other substances ranging from carrier oils like sweet almond oils to artificial substances like chemicals or synthetic fragrances.

Different essential oils command different rates. If a company sells all its 5ml bottles of essential oils at the same price – regardless of the kind of essential oils they contain -- there is something not quite right here. The oils are likely to have been adulterated one way or the other.

These oils are of a lower quality as they contain chemicals and other synthetic substances. Experts in the field strongly advice choosing oils that are genuine – pure and unadulterated by other additives. You extract the most benefits from 100% pure essential oils. You want the purest – the best – that you can get your hands on for your dearest pet dog.

Quality generally commands price. However, because your dog also reaps the most advantage from high-quality essential oils, you get real value for your money. Do not give in to the temptation to buy essential oils that come at a ridiculously low price. They are likely to be of poorer quality. Real quality has a price. Make sure to buy wisely – choosing essential oils that will give your beloved dog real comfort and relief.

Chapter 5 – Essential Oils and What they can do for your Beloved Pet Dog

Essential oils are recognized as being helpful in addressing a rather substantial range of problems. However, you have to know what particular essential oils to use for specific situations.

The following is a quick rundown of essential oils and what they are good for.

Thyme, pine, myrrh and eucalyptus help in treating cough and other respiratory problems.

Sweet fennel, chamomile and peppermint work best to ease motion sickness and nausea.

If your dog has arthritis, you can help ease his pain with rosemary and lavender, sandalwood, thyme, pine, or birch.

Lavender and marjoram give relief for sore over-used muscles.

Tea tree, peppermint with rosemary, and patchouli with myrrh give relief for dry, itchy, and sensitive skin.

Patchouli with myrrh is good for bruises, scrapes, and cuts.

Peppermint helps address flatulence.

Citronella with lemongrass, peppermint, pine, cedar wood and eucalyptus work best to repel insects.

To calm and relax your hyperactive pet, you can use marjoram, lemon, chamomile, jasmine, lavender, frankincense, bergamot, or ylang ylang.

Ylang Ylang and sandalwood help to reduce aggression.

Orange blossom, bergamot and basil help your dog recover from grief.

It also helps to know the properties of major essential oils to better understand why their use is recommended for certain conditions.

Bergamot has soothing and antifungal properties. It is excellent for treating infections triggered by bacterial or yeast overgrowth.

Carrot Seed is a tonic; it promotes healing by stimulating tissue to regenerate. It rejuvenates skin, moisturizing it and keeping it hydrated. It also has anti-inflammatory and antibacterial properties.

Cedar wood has antiseptic properties. It helps your dog repel fleas. It also stimulates blood circulation. It conditions your dog's skin and coat.

Chamomile German is non-toxic, safe and gentle for use. It is good for treating burns, allergies and skin irritation.

Chamomile Roman calms the nerves. It is an analgesic; it also has antispasmodic properties. As such, it helps relieve teething discomforts, cramps and muscle pain.

Clary Sage calms the nerve. It helps soothe your pet, quieting his nerves so he does not get extremely agitated.

Eucalyptus Radiata is an expectorant. It has anti-inflammatory and antiviral properties. It helps decongest your pet's chest, allowing him to breathe easily.

Geranium is mild and gentle. Its antifungal properties help clear ear infections. Geranium helps your pet to fend off ticks.

Ginger is safe – non-irritating and non-toxic. It helps your dog digest his food efficiently. It is also good for relieving symptoms of motion sickness. It relieves pain associated with arthritis and sprains.

Helichrysum has strong therapeutic properties. It acts as an analgesic and anti-inflammatory agent. It has regenerative properties. It makes bruises heal fast. It helps calm skin irritation.

Lavender is mild, gentle and safe to use. It calms the nerves. It soothes skin irritation. It is generally effective for common ailments that may affect your pet dog.

Sweet marjoram relaxes stiff muscles. It has calming effects and strong antibacterial properties. It hastens healing of wounds and skin infections.

Peppermint has antispasmodic properties. It repels insects. It also stimulates blood circulation. It relieves pain associated with sprains and arthritis. Combined with ginger, it helps with motion sickness.

Sweet orange helps your dog repel fleas. It also keeps your dog sweet-smelling.

Valerian soothes the nerves. It helps your dog overcome anxiety.

Chapter 6 – Essential Oils Recipes for your Pet Dog

Essential oils recipes are simple and easy to prepare, and they are highly effective if you want to treat your pet for common problems that affect his health and disposition. If your dog has a problem with ticks and fleas, skin irritation, motion sickness, anxiety, hyperactivity, and more, you may just be surprised by how much these recipes using essential oils can help him.

Prepare dark-colored glass bottles to store these essential oil blends in after you make them. Make sure to label each bottle carefully, putting down the name of the essential oil blends and the date when you made them.

You will discover that these recipes are safe, mild and gentle on your dog. As with all topical medications, however, it pays to be careful. Do not apply the oils right away without doing a patch test. Simply take a drop of the blend and rub it on a small area on your dog's armpit. Choose an area that is sparsely covered with fur so you can easily see signs of irritation. These signs (redness, itchiness, inflammation) will usually become apparent after 24 hours. Do not use the blend if your dog shows adverse reactions to it.

Essential Oils Recipe for Motion Sickness

Is your pet dog prone to motion sickness? Address the problem with the following essential oils recipe for motion sickness. It will soothe him, make him less dizzy, calm his stomach and make him less nauseous.

Use 120 ml or 4oz. of base oil. Blend in 10 drops of Peppermint (scientific name: Mentha piperita) and 14 drops of Ginger (scientific name: Zingiber officinale).

Apply the essential oils blend on your dog, specifically on his belly, under his armpit, and on the inner tip of his ears.

You can also use a variation of the diffuser and inhalation method. Dab a cotton ball with some drops and put it right in front of the car's air vent. This will allow the soothing essential oils fragrance to circulate in the vehicle and ease the symptoms of motion sickness – making the ride more comfortable for both you and your beloved pet.

Essential Oils Recipe for Arthritis

Is your pet dog suffering from arthritis? One or more of his joints may be inflamed, causing them to become stiff and painful to move. This condition usually worsens as your dog advances in age.

Relieve your dog of some of his pain by using this effective essential oils recipe. In 120 ml or 4oz. of base oil, blend in the following essential oils: 7 drops of Valerian (scientific name: Valeriana officinalis), 5 drops of Ginger (scientific name: Zingiber officinale), 4 drops of Peppermint (scientific name: Mentha piperita), and 8 drops of

Helichrysum (scientific name: Helichrysum italicum).

As an alternative, you can also use this. In 120 ml or 4oz. of base oil, blend in the following essential oils: 8 of drops Ginger (scientific name: Zingiber officinale), 6 drops of Lavender (scientific name: Lavandula angustifolia), and 8 drops of Lemon oil (scientific name: Citrus limon)

Put a few drops of the blend into your hands. Gently massage your pet's painful joints, talking to him in calm, gentle and soothing voice.

Essential Oils Recipe to Use as Tick Repellent

Ticks simply cannot withstand lavender, bay and geranium. Use this knowledge to concoct a tick repellent using the essential oils of the aforementioned plants and keep those ticks at bay.

To 120 ml or 4oz of base oil, add the following: 6 drops of Lemon Eucalyptus (scientific name: Eucalyptus Citriodora), 8 drops of Geranium (scientific name: Pelargonium graveolens) and 10 drops of Lavender (scientific name: Lavandula angustifolia). Apply some drops to your dog, in areas most susceptible to ticks – tail, legs, chest, back and neck.

Essential Oils Recipe to Repel Flea

Use 4 oz. of any base oil or 240 ml or 8 oz. all-natural shampoo as base. Add 5 to 7 drops of Peppermint (scientific name: Mentha piperita), 4 drops of Citronella (scientific name: Cymbopogon nardus), 2 to 5 drops of Clary Sage (scientific name: Salvia sclarea), and 2 to 4 drops of Lemon (Citrus limon).

Make a fragrant flea collar by putting a few drops of this blend on the bandanna or cotton collar of your pet dog. Use as a flea repellent by applying some drops of the blend on your dog's tail, legs, back, chest and neck.

Essential Oils Recipe for Skin Irritations

Does your dog suffer from skin problems? Is he usually beset by bouts of discomfort from itchiness? If so, lose no time to give him relief. Make the following essential oils recipe, apply it on the affected prickly areas and soothe your beloved pet.

Use the following essential oils: 6 drops of Carrot Seed (scientific name: Daucus carota), 6 drops of Chamomile, German (scientific name: Matricaria recutita), 5 drops of Geranium (scientific name: Pelargonium graveolens), and 7 drops of Lavender (scientific name: Lavandula angustifolia). Add the drops to 240 ml or 8 oz. of shampoo made from all-natural ingredients to make a gentle and calming shampoo. Or, you can add the oils to 4 oz. of your preferred base oil to make a topical balm for scratchy skin. Apply on irritated areas.

Essential Oils Recipe for Ear Infections

Of course, you want to keep your dog free from ear infections. Apply this blend to help prevent and treat infections.

Use 120 ml or 4 oz. of base oil (jojoba, olive oil, or sweet almond oil are good choices). Add the following essential oils - - 6 drops of Chamomile, Roman (scientific name: Anthemis nobilis), 5 drops of Niaouli (scientific name: Melaleuca quinquenervia viridiflora), 8 drops of Lavender (scientific name: Lavandula angustifolia), and 5 drops of Bergamot (scientific name: Citrus bergamia).

Using a dropper, apply a few drops of the blend inside your dog's ear while massaging his outer ear. Use a cotton ball to clean his ear. The oil blend will loosen and prod out the filth inside his ear, rendering the ear less susceptible to infection. If the ear is already infected, the Lavender and Niaouli have anti-viral and antibacterial properties to hasten the healing process.

Here is an alternative recipe for ear infection. Mix 5 drops each of geranium, melaleuca, and lavender with 1 tablespoon of coconut oil. Clean your dog's ear using a natural cleaner then apply the essential oil mixture using a Q-tip to gently rub it in. Do this twice every day and watch the ear infection clear up fast.

Essential Oils Recipe for Body Odor

Do you want your dog to smell clean and fresh? Just make this recipe and you are certain to enjoy cuddling your pet more often.

Use your favorite 240 ml. or 8 oz all-natural shampoo. Simply add 3 drops of Sweet Marjoram (scientific name: Origanum majorana), 4 drops of Geranium (scientific name: Pelargonium graveolens), 4 drops of Chamomile Roman (Anthemis nobilis), and 7 to 8 drops of Lavender (scientific name: Lavandula angustifolia).

If your dog smells unusually bad (even your well-loved pet may sometimes smell this way, particularly on really humid days!), try this quick and easy essential oils recipe. Use 1 cup of distilled water and add the following: 3 drops of Eucalyptus (scientific name: Eucalyptus radiata), 6 drops of Peppermint (scientific name: Mentha piperita), 6 drops of Sweet Orange (scientific name: Citrus sinensis), and 10 drops Lavender (scientific name: Lavandula angustifolia). Allow the oils and water to combine by shaking vigorously in a spray bottle.

Spray the blend on your dog's body. Avoid spraying in the direction of his head; cover his eyes and face to make sure that you do not get any of the blend on them.

This is a lovely and refreshing recipe. The lavender and eucalyptus have antibacterial properties that will keep your dog clean and germ-free. You can also use this blend to spray your room with, giving it a garden-fresh scent that you and your dog will simply love.

Essential Oils Recipe for Anxiety

Your dog may become anxious for certain reasons. He may fear being separated from you. He may shy away from going to new places or interacting with new people or other animals. He may become alarmed by any unusual noise. You can ease his anxiety by using the following essential oils recipe.

In 120 ml or 4 oz. of base oil (sweet almond, jojoba, or olive oil works well), mix 6 to 8 drops of Valerian (scientific name: Valeriana officinalis), 6 to 8 drops of Lavender (scientific name: Lavandula angustifolia), 3 to 4 drops of Clary Sage (scientific name: Salvia sclarea) and 3 to 4 drops of Sweet Marjoram (scientific name: Origanum majorana).

Apply this blend topically on your pet dog. Rub about 3 drops of the blend between your palms then massage your dog. Apply it under his armpits, on his inner thighs, or on the tips of his ears.

Another option is to make a lavender powder to help your dog overcome his anxiety. You can use corn starch, rice flour, or baking soda as base for this recipe.

Prepare a blend of the following essential oils – 1 part of Ylang Ylang (scientific name: Cananga odorata), 2 parts of Bergamot (scientific name: Citrus bergamia), 2 parts of Clary Sage (scientific name: Salvia sclarea), and 3 parts of Lavender (scientific name: Lavandula angustifolia). For every cup of baking soda (you may use one cup of a mix of rice flour and baking soda instead), stir in 12 to 15 drops of the essential oil blend. Mix well.

If your dog finds a car ride to his veterinarian stressful, a blanket sprinkled with this powder and placed inside the cage is likely to have a calming effect on him. If your dog shows clear signs of anxiety every time you leave him at home, you can try sprinkling the powder on a dress you have already used and put this dress on his bed. Your pet will find it reassuring to sense your smell. The oil blend will calm and relax him so that he becomes significantly less anxious and fretful when you are away.

Essential Oils Recipe for Hyperactivity

Is your dog hyperactive? Does he sometimes show the tendency to be abnormally active and disruptive? If so, the following recipe can help calm him down and rein in hyperactivity.

In 120 ml or 4 oz. of base oil (jojoba, sweet almond, jojoba, or olive oil are popular options), mix 6 drops of Lavender (scientific name: Lavandula angustifolia), 3 drops of Bergamot (scientific name: Citrus bergamia), 6 drops of Valerian (scientific name: Valeriana officinalis), 4 drops of Sweet Marjoram (scientific name: Origanum majorana), and 5 drops Chamomile, Roman (scientific name: Anthmis nobilis).

Apply as you would the recipe for anxiety – massaging the blend in the same areas – inner thighs, armpits, between the toes and on the tips of his ears.

Conclusion

Thank you again for downloading this book!

I hope this book was able to help you understand and appreciate the many uses of essential oils that your dog can benefit from.

The next step is to put your knowledge to practical use. Get high-quality essential oils, prepare the simple, easy-to-prepare essential oils recipes and see your dog enjoy their therapeutic and healing properties.

Finally, if you enjoyed this book, then I'd like to ask you for a favor, would you be kind enough to leave a review for this book on Amazon? It'd be greatly appreciated!

Thank you and good luck!

Made in the USA
Middletown, DE
07 December 2015